STARTING OUT

baby HAMSTERS

LAURA K. MURRAY

CREATIVE EDUCATION • CREATIVE PAPERBACKS

CONT

ENTS

I AM A PUP.

I am a baby hamster.

Look at my
small nose!

I was born without hair. I couldn't see or hear. After one week, my hair started to grow.

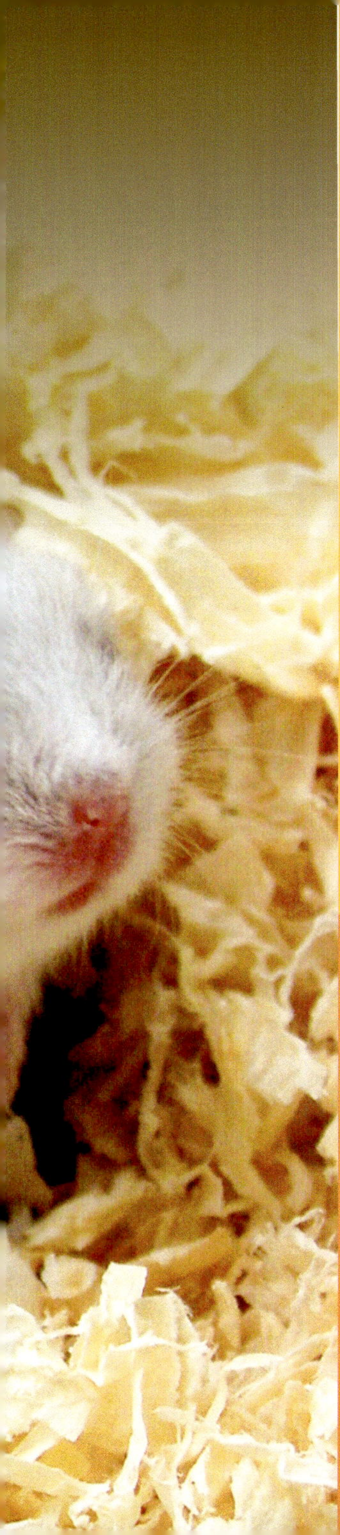

At two weeks old, my eyes and ears opened. I drank my mother's milk until I was one month old.

My water bottle has a tip

Pellets are my main meals. I hide treats inside my cheeks. They have big pouches.

My teeth
keep growing.

I love to exercise on my wheel!

I'm active at night and sleep during the day. People should hold me gently.

Being a hamster is the best!

SPEAK AND LISTEN

EAK!

Can you speak like a pup? Hamsters may squeak, click, and chirp.

Listen to these sounds:

Now it is your turn!

PUP WORDS

active: being awake, playing, and moving

exercise: movement to keep the body healthy and strong

pellet: a small, hard piece of food for pets

pouch: a pocket-like space in an animal's cheek that can be used to store food

READING CORNER

Greenwood, Nancy. *My Pet Hamster*. New York: Gareth Stevens, 2023.

Hansen, Grace. *Hamsters in the Wild!* Minneapolis: Pop!, 2025.

Rossiter, Brienna. *My Pet Hamster*. Mendota Heights, Minn.: Little Blue House, 2022.

INDEX

PUBLISHED BY CREATIVE EDUCATION AND CREATIVE PAPERBACKS
P.O. Box 227, Mankato, Minnesota 56002
Creative Education and Creative Paperbacks are imprints of The Creative Company
www.thecreativecompany.us

LIBRARY OF CONGRESS CATALOGING-IN-PUBLICATION DATA
Names: Murray, Laura K., 1989- author
Title: Baby hamsters / by Laura K. Murray.
Description: Mankato, Minnesota : Creative Education and Creative Paperbacks, [2026] | Series: Starting out | Includes bibliographical references and index. | Audience: Ages 4-7 | Audience: Grades K-1 | Summary: "Introduce beginning readers to the world of baby hamsters with this life science starter. Includes photos, a labeled animal diagram, "Speak and Listen" section, glossary, and further resources"-- Provided by publisher.
Identifiers: LCCN 2025015257 (print) | LCCN 2025015258 (ebook) | ISBN 9798895810330 library binding | ISBN 9781682779866 paperback | ISBN 9798895811597 ebook
Subjects: LCSH: Hamsters as pets--Juvenile literature | Hamsters--Juvenile literature
Classification: LCC SF459.H3 M874 2026 (print) | LCC SF459.H3 (ebook) | DDC 636.935/6--dc23/eng/20250728
LC record available at https://lccn.loc.gov/2025015257
LC ebook record available at https://lccn.loc.gov/2025015258

DESIGN AND PRODUCTION
Design by Rhea Magaro
Art direction by Tom Morgan

PHOTOGRAPHS BY
Dreamstime/Irina Orlova, 10, Isselee, 12, Joanne Zhe, 6, Lepas, 7, 14; Freepik/tsekhmister, cover; Getty Images/retales botijero, 9; Shutterstock/Elya Vatel, 11, jerrysa, 5, Lepas, 2, Monika_1, 8; Unsplash/Ricky Kharawala, 4

Printed in the United States